Christmas 2005

Happy reading!

from
Sue, Rick, Sarah & Keith (Churchill)

x x x x

CATS

EDITED BY MARGARET LANNAMANN

DESIGNED BY DIANE HOBBING

Ariel Books

**Andrews McMeel
Publishing**

Kansas City

CATS

ISBN: 0-7407-3365-6
Library of Congress Catalog Card Number:
2002111878

CATS

Introduction

They want to come in, they want to go out, they're **hungry,** they're not hungry—the only predictable thing about cats is their unpredictability. When you call, they might come running, but they might just as easily **ignore** you completely. One moment you're struck by their elegance as they **pose** on the

windowsill; the next moment you're laughing as they play with a discarded gift bow or peek out of a paper bag.

There's no doubt about it, cats have

their own agendas. But we love them anyway, and have for thousands of years. **Mysterious,** beautiful, and just a little bit elusive, cats fascinate us—and probably always will.

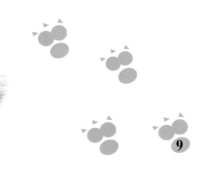

PLAYTIME

Favorite cat **toys** include paper bags, Christmas tree ornaments (usually the antique, breakable kind), lace table-cloths, balled-up bits of aluminum foil, gift bows, and boxes big enough for climbing in.

Cats think about three things: food, sex, and nothing.

—Adair Lara

A LICK AND A PROMISE

When cats **lick** their fur with their raspy tongues, they separate any hairs that may be stuck together. When the hairs are separated instead of matted, their coats do a **better** job of retaining heat.

I just **wish** my companion animal would think of me as his companion animal instead of thinking of me as his butler.

—Bill Hall

ALL'S WELL WITH THE WORLD

When your cat **blinks,** she is in a **peaceful** and contented mood.

All I need to know I
learned
from my cat.

—Suzy Becker

2 1

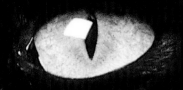

A rat's **night vision** is ten times superior to that of a human's.

Its tail was a plume of such magnificence that it almost wore the cat.

—Hugh Leonard

Every
life
should
have
nine
cats.
—Unknown

va**CAT**ion

According to a recent **survey,** 16 percent of cat owners take their **pets** on vacation with them, and 8 percent of owners take their **cats** to work with them!

C A T S

FREE-WHEELING

Those little wheels on suitcases have
made traveling easier for millions of
people. Now the same idea has been
adapted to a **cat carryall,** so you can
roll your pet to the train, the plane, or
even just to the vet.

A cat is an enigma but . . . a very successful enigma.

—Jeremy Angel

The things on a cat's mind
must be **wonderful**
beyond imagining.

—Roger Caras

HOLD THE MOO JUICE

Contrary to popular belief, **cats shouldn't** drink milk, as it can upset their digestive systems.

C A T S

WEIGH IN

Cats **weigh** an average of **eleven** pounds.

If a cat **spoke,** it would say things like "Hey, I don't see the *problem* here."

—Roy Blount Jr.

ANCIENT TRADITION

In ancient **Egypt,** cat owners would shave off their eyebrows to **mourn** the death of their beloved pet.

CATS

TRY A LITTLE TENDERNESS

Consider **volunteering** at your local animal shelter. The **cats** who are confined there will **greatly** appreciate your **effort** and **love.**

A **tail** held straight out behind a cat means that the **cat** is about to **attack,** say the experts. If it is expressing itself **loudly** in cat language at the same time, it means you have **shut** its tail in the door.

—John Tickner

It's **true** that living alone for years makes you eccentric. I talk to my cat. Why lie? Over the years I've developed the habit of *actually answering myself, in the cat's voice* (or what I imagine her voice to be).

—Stephanie Brush

THE NOSE *DOESN'T* KNOW

The **myth** that by **feeling** your cat's **nose** you can tell whether or not she is **sick** is just that: a myth. A damp nose has **nothing** to do with overall health.

Cats are intended to teach us that **not everything** in nature has a function.

—Garrison Keillor

A **black cat** dropped
soundlessly from a high wall,
like a spoonful of dark treacle,
and melted under a gate.

—Elizabeth Lemarchand

Cats seem to go on the principle that it never does any harm to **ask** for what **you want.**

—Joseph Wood Krutch

CYBER KITTY

Felix is busy surfing the web these days.
Visit **www.catslikefelix.com,** and
you can download him onto your PC,
where he will run and jump around your
screen. His toys include a ball of string
and a wind-up mouse.

5 3

You enter into a certain amount of **madness** when you marry a person with pets.

—Nora Ephron

Cats invented self-esteem. —Erma Bombeck

LUCK OF THE BRITISH?

In **England,** it is considered **lucky** to have a **black** cat.

SIPPIN' PRETTY

Cats **drink** water by
lapping three or
four times and then
swallowing what
they have lapped up.

Oh, the cats in this town have their secrets. —Mary Virginia Micka

The phrase "domesticated cat" is an **oxymoron.**

—George F. Will

MOM-TO-BE

A female **cat** is **pregnant** for sixty-five to seventy days before giving birth.

Cats have a

consuming

passion for

watching

human beings.

—Akif Pirinçci and

Rolf Degen

BREATHE EASY

Domestic cats can **purr** as they breathe in **and** as they breathe out. **Big** cats like lions and tigers can only **purr** as they breathe out.

FEEDING FRENZY

In a recent **survey,** 88 percent of cat owners say they **feed** their cat dried food, 40 percent feed canned food, and about 15 percent feed table scraps.

In **truth,** most
of us don't know
our cats.

—Elizabeth Marshall
Thomas

EAR YE, EAR YE

Cats have **thirty-two** muscles that control the movement of their ears.

SOUTHPAWS

Cats, like people, can be **either** right- or left-handed.

There is always time for a nap.

—Suzy Becker

Spot illustrations by Lisa Parett

Book design and composition
by Diane Hobbing of
Snap-Haus Graphics
in Dumont, NJ